GEORGE WASHINGTON CARVER

PEANUT WIZARD

BY LAURA DRISCOLL

illustrated by Jill Weber

Grosset & Dunlap · New York

For Jane O'Connor and Megan Bryant—
two fantastic editors I wouldn't trade for nuttin'!—L.D.

To Cameron—my peanut-butter-eating model—J.W.

Library of Congress Cataloging-in-Publication Data is available.

ISBN 978-0-448-43243-4 (pbk)   O P Q R S T

ISBN 978-0-448-43286-1 (GB)   A B C D E F G H I J

From the desk of

Ms. Brandt

Dear Class,

Now that we have learned about some famous scientists, I am so eager to read your reports and find out who was your favorite.

- Did your scientist find out something new, something that nobody had known about?

- How did your scientist make his or her discovery?

- Often scientists make discoveries by doing experiments. Did you do an experiment for your report? If you did, what did you discover?

Have fun doing your report.

Ms. Brandt

I'm NUTS about peanuts and peanut butter. If I could, I would eat peanut butter for breakfast, lunch, and dinner. But 150 years ago, people didn't like to eat peanuts very much. They were mostly used to feed animals. Then along came a scientist named George Washington Carver. My mom and I saw a TV show about him. His nickname was "the Peanut Wizard." (Once I heard that, I <u>had</u> to find out more about him.) He showed the world that peanuts were yummy and could be used in lots of recipes. He also showed how peanuts could be made into many useful things.

Guess which one of these things is not made from peanuts?

TURF BUILDER

DOG TREATS

BEST Peanut Butter

JAM

SOAP

ANSWER: jam

Here is GEORGE WASHINGTON CARVER holding a peanut plant.

mmm good!

Now the average American eats more than six pounds of peanuts and peanut butter every year. (I guess I'm not the average American because I bet I eat way more than that.) November is Peanut Butter Lovers month. And guess what! My birthday is November 12th.

Here is me, eating peanut butter, the best stuff on Earth.

A SAD BEGINNING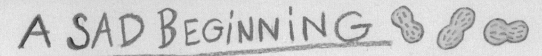

This is the Carver farm where George grew up. It's in Diamond Grove, Missouri. I'd like to go there someday.

George Washington Carver did not start out as a famous scientist. He started out as just George. He was born around 1864 on a farm in Missouri that was owned by Susan and Moses Carver. George was a slave. That meant he was <u>owned</u> by the Carvers. So were his mother and his older brother, Jim. It makes me sad and mad to think there was a time in America when people could own other people.

GEORGE'S MOTHER

GEORGE

JIM

It makes me even sadder what happened to George's mother. Slave robbers took her. These were men who kidnapped slaves so they could sell them to somebody else. George and Jim never saw their mother again. Even though the Carvers had owned slaves, they sound like pretty nice people. They raised George and his brother. And they treated them like they were their sons. George was smaller and got sick a lot, so he helped Susan Carver with the housework and in the garden.

Slavery ended in 1865 when George was still a baby.

THE PLANT DOCTOR

What George liked best was working in Susan's garden.
He wanted to know all about different plants. He was very curious.
That is something a good scientist needs to be!

I don't know what plants George grew in his garden. I cut out pictures of plants and flowers that we grow in ours.

THE DOCTOR
is in!

George also had a secret plant hospital in the woods. He took sick plants there and tried to make them better. People started calling him "the Plant Doctor."

THE PLANT ARTIST.

George liked to draw plants too. He'd look very carefully at the shape of the leaves and the flowers. Like you told us in class, Ms. Brandt, scientists learn by looking. With paints that he made from berry juice, George also painted flowers on rocks.

FLOWER

PETAL

BIGGER BUD

BUD

LEAF

STEMS

ROOTS

Here is my drawing of a daisy plant.

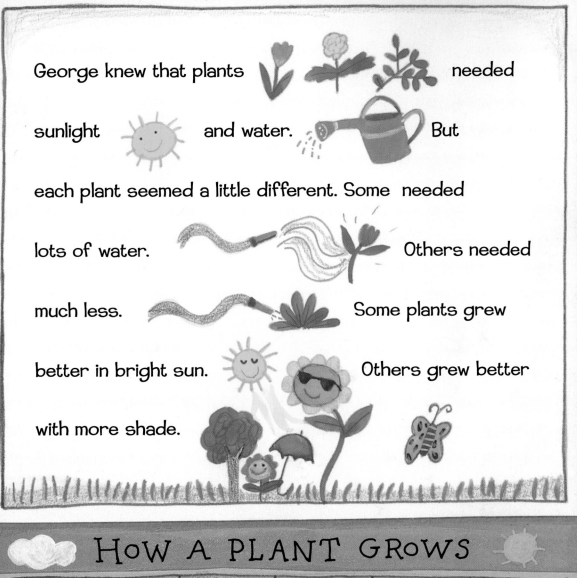

George knew that plants needed sunlight and water. But each plant seemed a little different. Some needed lots of water. Others needed much less. Some plants grew better in bright sun. Others grew better with more shade.

HOW A PLANT GROWS

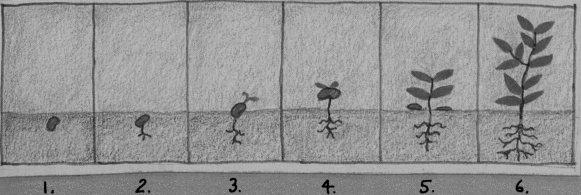

1.   2.   3.   4.   5.   6.

Lots of Questions

There were some plants that George couldn't figure out. He wondered why some plants died even if they got plenty of light and water.

What am I doing wrong?

Here are two of our houseplants.

This one just grows and grows.

I'm still trying to figure out what to do for this poor plant.

As George got older, he had more and more questions about the world. But Susan and Moses Carver couldn't answer all George's questions. George needed to go to school. However, because he was black, George couldn't go to the school near his home. It was for white kids only. The school for black children was eight miles away. So do you know what George did? He packed up and went to the new town, all by himself. He was only about twelve.

Although George learned a lot at the school, the teacher could not answer all his questions about nature. So when George heard about a better black school in another town, off he went. George moved many times. He went to lots of black schools in lots of towns.

In some towns, he found families to live with.
Or he found a job and lived on his own.

He did jobs like cooking,   washing clothes,

ironing,

and pitching hay.

He did all that just so he could go to school and learn.

Here are my jobs:
Make bed. Walk the dog. Take
out trash. Clear table.

WOOF

GEORGE GETS THE DIRT ON DIRT

When George was about thirty years old, he started college. It was his big dream. Now he could find answers to his questions about plants. He learned about soil and how important it is, since a plant gets its food from the soil. He learned that some kinds of soils have more vitamins—or nutrients.

By the time George finished school, the teachers thought he knew more about plants than they did. They asked him to stay and work there. And he did.

DIRTY WORDS

soil - dirt, the top layer of the earth where plants grow

mulch - wood chips put on top of soil to keep moisture in, to keep plant roots from freezing, and to keep weeds away

fertilizer - anything you add to soil to help plants grow

manure - animal poop (sounds gross but it's a really good fertilizer!)

compost - fertilizer made from mixing dirt and rotting stuff (like food scraps and leaves)

We have a compost heap. We put in eggshells, food scraps, even rabbit doo-doo along with some dirt. After a while, everything breaks down and the dirt becomes fertilizer.

We use it in our garden.

A DIRTY EXPERIMENT

What kind of soil is best for growing plants? I did an experiment to find out. Here's what I used: three lima beans, three plastic cups, potting soil, sand, water, liquid plant food.

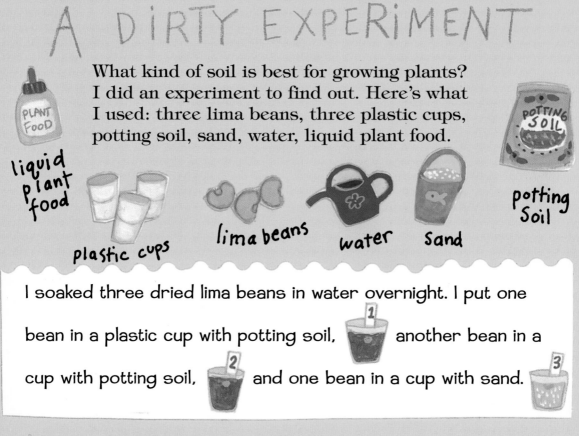

liquid plant food

plastic cups

lima beans

water

Sand

potting Soil

I soaked three dried lima beans in water overnight. I put one bean in a plastic cup with potting soil, another bean in a cup with potting soil, and one bean in a cup with sand.

I buried the beans about 2 inches deep in the soil or sand. I poured ½ cup water into each cup every day for 10 days. The water for #1 always had 5 drops of liquid plant food in it. The water for #2 and #3 was just plain water. I set all three cups on a sunny windowsill.

I made a prediction. (That's when scientists say what they think will happen in an experiment.) I predicted that #1 would grow best because it was in soil (which has vitamins) and also got extra vitamins from the plant food. I thought #2 would be next best because it was in soil (with vitamins) but didn't have plant food. And I thought #3 would have the hardest time growing because it was in sand, which doesn't have a lot of vitamins in it.

So! WAS I RIGHT OR WRONG?

Well, I was both right and wrong about my predictions. #1 did grow the best. But #2 didn't grow at all!

I called a plant store near my house. The lady there told me some interesting stuff about beans.

Bean Fact: When a bean plant is first sprouting, it gets all the food it needs right from the bean, not the soil. It only starts to get vitamins from the soil after the food stored in the bean is all used up. That is about seven days.

Interesting, but that still didn't explain why #2 didn't sprout at all.

another BEAN FACT: Some beans are just duds and don't sprout.

Aha! Maybe #2 was a dud bean. Next time, I will plant two or three beans in each pot in case one is a dud. I will also do the experiment for twenty days, not ten, to see how much plant food helps the plant grow after it has used up all the food in the bean.

CONCLUSION: My dirty experiment didn't go the way I thought it would. But I learned some stuff about beans!

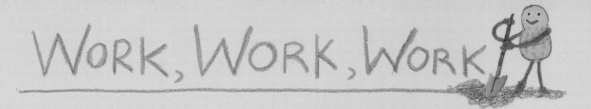

Then, one day, George got a letter from a man named Booker T. Washington. He was the head of a new black college in Alabama called Tuskegee Institute. Booker T. Washington wanted George Washington Carver to teach everything he knew about plants—not just to students but to farmers too. So George said yes. If he taught farmers how to grow better crops, they could make more money.

BOOKER T. WASHINGTON

I'm coming!

GEORGE WASHINGTON CARVER

When George Washington Carver arrived at Tuskegee Institute, he got a surprise. There were hardly any buildings.

Besides teaching school, George needed to help build the school!

So, where's the rest of the school?

Um, it's going to be over there.

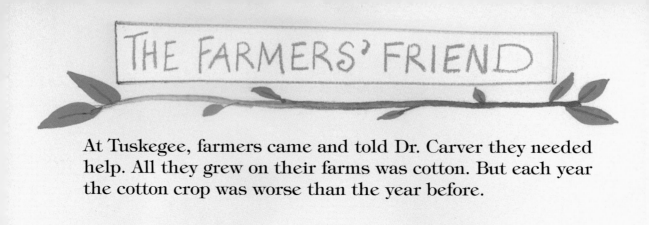

THE FARMERS' FRIEND

At Tuskegee, farmers came and told Dr. Carver they needed help. All they grew on their farms was cotton. But each year the cotton crop was worse than the year before.

The plant doctor knew why. Planting nothing but cotton was taking too much good stuff, like nitrogen, out of the soil. It was as if the soil had no vitamins left in it.

SCHOOL ON WHEELS

Some farmers couldn't come to Tuskegee to hear George Washington Carver. So on weekends, Dr. Carver took the school to them. He built a special wagon. He loaded it with sweet potatoes and peanuts and black-eyed peas. Then he drove around to the farms.

Dr. Carver told the farmers to grow different things. Things like sweet potatoes and peanuts! Why? Because these crops put nitrogen back in the soil. Once there was enough nitrogen in the soil, the farmers could grow cotton again. Good cotton! This idea is called <u>crop rotation</u>. If you plant a different crop each year, the soil gets healthier.

PEANUT PLANT

The farmers listened to Dr. Carver. They grew lots of peanuts and sweet potatoes. But then they had trouble selling them. People didn't want them as much as they wanted cotton. What would the farmers do now?

S P U D S

SWEET POTATO

Dr. Carver wasn't discouraged. He did some work in his lab. He started thinking up new ways to use the sweet potato. Then he did the same thing for the peanut. Do you know what he made? All the things on this page . . . and hundreds more!

George Washington Carver working in his lab

= SOFT HANDS — hand lotion

shampoo

GLUE — glue

paint

GET CLEAN Laundry SOAP — laundry soap

coffee

THE PEANUT FEAST

But Dr. Carver still had to convince people that foods made from peanuts were yummy. He came up with a great idea. One day he invited businessmen over for lunch. He and his students served them a big fancy meal. The businessmen loved it.

After dessert, Dr. Carver had a surprise for his guests. Everything on the menu was made from peanuts! I wish I had been there.

GEORGE'S MENU

BREAD
SOUP
"CHICKEN" LOAF
CREAMED
VEGETABLES
iCE CREAM
☆ COOKIES ☆

Everything's delicious!

Best chicken I ever ate!

Now the businessmen were convinced—peanut growing could be a big business.

For my favorite peanut dessert... TURN THE PAGE

MY FAVORITE PEANUT BUTTER DESSERT

* You'll See Why!

CHOCOLATE PEANUT BUTTER SMOOTHIE

<u>You will need:</u>

2 cups chocolate ice cream

2 cups milk

5 tablespoons creamy peanut butter

First, measure out the ice cream, put it in a big bowl, and leave it out to get soft. Add the milk and peanut butter. Mix everything together with a wooden spoon or whisk until smooth and creamy. Pour into a glass, add a straw, and sip!

Makes 3 big smoothies

This is really delicious. And for a dessert, it is pretty good for you. Peanuts are high in minerals like calcium, potassium, niacin, and magnesium. However, some people are very allergic to peanuts. Even a tiny taste of anything made with peanuts or peanut oil will make them sick.

George Washington Carver became famous. Newspapers wrote stories about him. But he kept on teaching at Tuskegee for forty-seven years. And that is where he is buried.

Here is Dr. Carver with President Franklin Roosevelt.

George Washington Carver could have become rich. But he wanted people to use what he discovered for free so they could make their lives better. On his gravestone it says: "He could have added fortune to fame, but caring for neither, he found happiness and honor in being helpful to the world."

That sounds about right to me!

A stamp with George's picture

SOME NUTTY FACTS

The world's largest peanut is 4 inches long!

Astronaut Alan B. Shepard, Jr. brought a peanut
with him to the moon!

In the U.S., creamy peanut butter sells better on the East Coast
and crunchy peanut butter sells better on the West Coast.

The average kid in America will eat 1,500 peanut butter
and jelly sandwiches before graduating from
high school . . . I think I've eaten that many already.

It takes about 540 peanuts to make a
12-ounce jar of peanut butter.

Annie-
George Washington Carver is one of my
heroes, too. Did you know that, even after
he became famous, he still couldn't go to
some hotels and restaurants just because
he was black? I certainly am glad that
things are different now.
Ms. Brandt